by Barbara A. Donovan
illustrated by Richard Torrey

Harcourt
SCHOOL PUBLISHERS

Copyright © by Harcourt, Inc.

All rights reserved. No part of this publication may be reproduced or transmitted in any form or by any means, electronic or mechanical, including photocopy, recording, or any information storage and retrieval system, without permission in writing from the publisher.

Requests for permission to make copies of any part of the work should be addressed to School Permissions and Copyrights, Harcourt, Inc., 6277 Sea Harbor Drive, Orlando, Florida 32887-6777. Fax: 407-345-2418.

HARCOURT and the Harcourt Logo are trademarks of Harcourt, Inc., registered in the United States of America and/or other jurisdictions.

Printed in the United States of America

ISBN 10: 0-15-351084-6
ISBN 13: 978-0-15-351084-7

Ordering Options
ISBN 10: 0-15-351084-6 (Grade 6 On-Level Collection)
ISBN 13: 978-0-15-351084-7 (Grade 6 On-Level Collection)
ISBN 10: 0-15-357980-3 (package of 5)
ISBN 13: 978-0-15-357980-6 (package of 5)

If you have received these materials as examination copies free of charge, Harcourt School Publishers retains title to the materials and they may not be resold. Resale of examination copies is strictly prohibited and is illegal.

Possession of this publication in print format does not entitle users to convert this publication, or any portion of it, into electronic format.

2 3 4 5 6 7 8 9 10   179   12 11 10 09 08 07

Paul's stomach flipped as he approached the door to his English class. He stood immobile, feeling clammy and sick, with his hand on the doorknob. He'd been dreading this day all year. He had hoped his teacher, Mr. Mars, would skip the chapter on making speeches, but on Friday, he'd told the class to preview those pages. Paul was a wreck. He couldn't make a speech in front of the class! His brain went haywire just thinking of the disasters that could occur.

Just as Paul was about to escape to the nurse's office, Jennifer Foley and her crowd of friends swarmed toward Paul. They swept him along with them into the classroom. Then Paul was set adrift as Jennifer and her pals followed the sinuous path between the desks to the corner of the classroom where they usually sat.

Paul made his solitary way to his own desk. He spotted Jake Watson leaning over Jennifer's shoulder. Jake was always jesting, and Jennifer laughed quietly at some joke that Jake had made.

Paul envied Jake's easy manner. Jake was an instant friend to everyone he met. It didn't matter if they were kids or adults, sports nuts like him or the brainiest kids in the school. Jake knew just what to say and when to say it. This was in direct contrast to Paul, who never knew what to say, so he hardly said anything at all.

Mr. Mars grabbed an open brown paper bag and began explaining what was in store for his English class. "Please pull one paper from the bag," he stated as he walked around the room. "On each paper is a number that shows the group that you'll be in for the next two weeks. You'll prepare and write your own speeches, and then you'll practice giving your speeches in your groups before giving them to the class."

Paul gulped and closed his eyes as he pulled a note from the bag—group six. Paul soon discovered that Jake, Jennifer, and Beth were in his group, too.

Mr. Mars went on to list what the elements of a good speech were. He also gave pointers about choosing topics for the speeches. Then he suggested that the groups briefly meet so that members could talk about things that interested them that might be interesting topics for their speeches.

Jake waved everyone over to his desk. Paul stood up nervously and proceeded to catch his foot on the leg of his desk. Luckily, he caught himself before he fell. He stumbled over to Jake's desk, feeling about as supple as the columns that hold up a roof. His face flamed, and he slid into the desk beside Jake's. Paul fumbled in his backpack to keep from looking at the others' faces.

Jake jump-started the discussion by talking about the thing he was most interested in at the moment—fly-fishing. Paul thought Jake's topic would be an interesting one for a speech, but he could sense that Jennifer and Beth thought it was boring. No one said a word to discourage Jake, though.

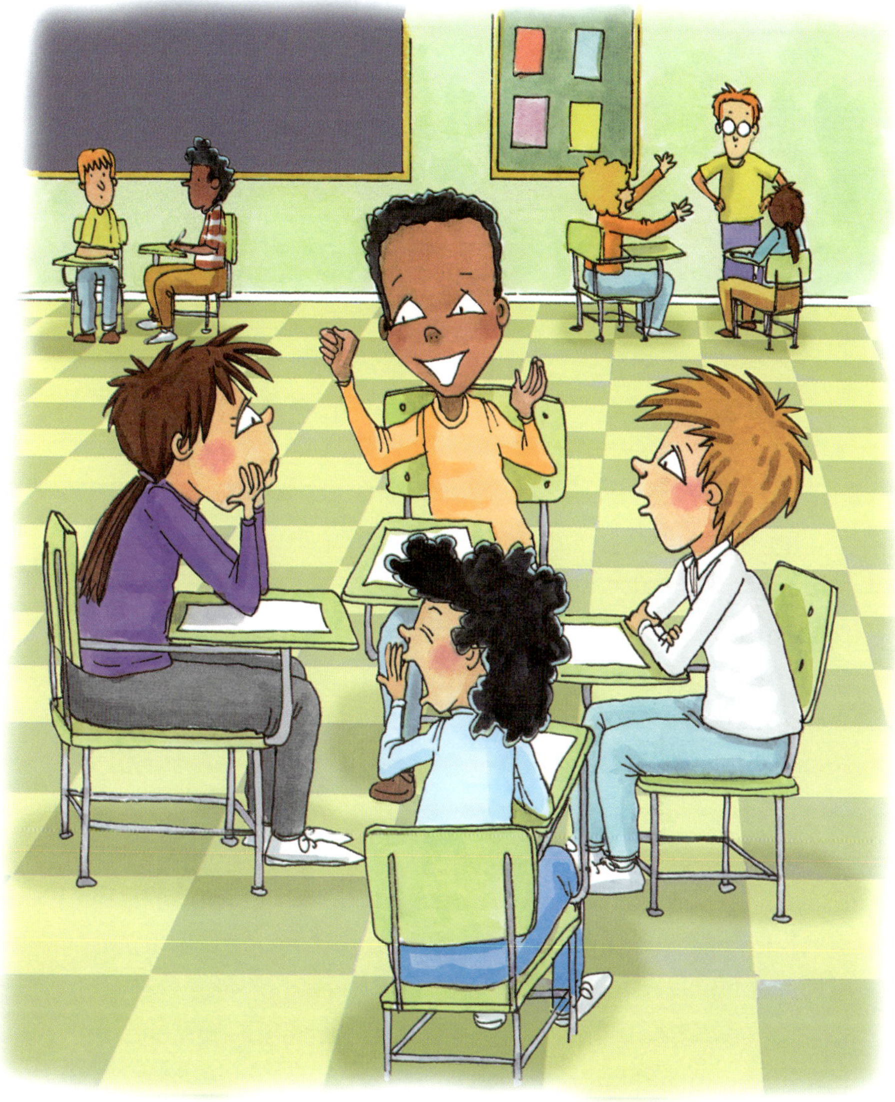

Jennifer shared her ideas next. The problem was that she had too many ideas. She was interested in writing poetry, but she didn't think that would be a good topic for a speech. She liked art, baseball, and tennis. She flitted from topic to topic. Paul was grateful to Jake for interrupting her long enough to invite Beth to contribute her ideas.

At first, Beth talked so quietly that they all sat on the edges of their seats straining to hear her. Then she started talking about her favorite topic—horror movies. Quiet, shy, retiring Beth loved to be scared. The scarier the movie, the better she liked it, and the louder and more confidently she spoke.

Only a few minutes remained in class for Paul to tell about his favorite things. Paul felt embarrassed to talk, as he usually did in a group. He stared at his hands, which were clenched tightly together on his desk, and he murmured that the thing he liked to do best was cook. He expected everyone to laugh at him, but they didn't. They did, however, start peppering him with questions about what he liked to cook, how he'd learned to cook, and whether he'd cook something for them.

When the bell finally rang, Paul was relieved. He hated being in the spotlight. Even though his group hadn't laughed at him yet, there was still time. Mr. Mars announced that tomorrow the groups would continue their brainstorming, choose topics for their speeches, and then narrow their topics.

The next day as Jake droned on about fly-fishing, Paul noticed that Jake even got Jennifer's and Beth's attention when he described what it was like to fish on a quiet lake early in the morning. Jennifer said he was almost poetic when he described the sky at sunrise, the clean air, and the cool lake waters. Jake's choice was clear. His speech would describe the feelings you get when fly-fishing.

Beth had already narrowed her topic. She decided that her speech would be a review of the latest horror movie she'd seen, *Attack of the Killer Grasshoppers*. Everyone in the group agreed that that topic seemed narrow enough.

Jennifer, on the other hand, was no closer to choosing a topic than she had been the day before. After about fifteen minutes, Paul gathered his courage and made a suggestion. He dug a packet of self-stick notes from his pocket and handed them to Jennifer.

He explained that when he was faced with tough choices, he wrote them on separate self-stick notes. First, he divided them into two lists—save and toss. Into the "save" list, he put his best ideas. The rest went into the "toss" list. Then, he'd stack all the notes in the toss list and put them aside. Next, he'd make new save-and-toss lists with only those ideas left in the save list. He'd keep doing this until there was only one self-stick note left in the save list.

Jennifer gave Paul's idea a try. At first, she had a difficult time putting any ideas in the toss list, but with the group's encouragement, she finally worked through the process. Her speech would be about adopting pets at the animal rescue center. Who would have guessed that that would be the one thing Jennifer felt most deeply about? Jennifer hadn't even known that about herself until she made her list.

When it was Paul's turn, he wrote his own save-and-toss list. He worked silently for a while, moving notes from one list to another. Finally, his save list had only two notes. He would talk about either his first time baking bread, which was a pretty funny story, or he'd explain the science behind why bread rises and root beer fizzles. He was about to put his baking-disaster story in the toss list, when Beth stopped him.

"I think kids would like your bread story," Beth said shyly. "I thought it was funny when you told about the dough sticking not only to your hands, but also to your arms up to your elbows, the refrigerator, the milk carton, and even the phone."

Paul smiled as he remembered, and then he said, "I'm worried that kids will be laughing at me instead of at my story."

Jake shook his head and said, "I don't think you have to worry. It's a funny story. We just have to work on how you present it. We'll work on your smile and your intonation when you speak."

"Yes," added Jennifer, "and we'll work on having you look into the audience's eyes so that you can connect with people. Maybe you could try giving your speech to yourself at home in a mirror. That's what I do when I want to practice reciting my poetry."

Paul, Beth, and Jake just stared at Jennifer. The image of Jennifer needing to practice anything stunned them all for a moment. Then they realized that they all needed help with some things and that they could help each other.

For the first time in his life, Paul was glad to be working in a group. He was starting to feel confident enough to share his ideas. Maybe by the time he had to give his speech, his tongue wouldn't feel fused to the roof of his mouth, and he'd actually be able to talk in front of the class. At least he knew he'd see three friendly faces in the audience.

Think Critically

1. How would you describe Paul's character?
2. Summarize this story in a few sentences.
3. Why is Jake so likable?
4. Will Paul be able to make his speech in front of the class or will he be too nervous? Give reasons to support your answer.
5. Which of the students in the group—Paul, Jake, Jennifer, or Beth—has personality qualities closest to yours? Explain your answer.

Performing Arts

Tips for Public Speaking Make a list of tips that Paul could follow to help him when it comes to giving his speech in front of his class. Your list might include tips on how to stand, speak clearly, and use gestures effectively.

School-Home Connection Tell a family member about Paul's problem and how he solved it. Then discuss your own experiences with speaking or performing in public.

Word Count: 1,434